# UNDERSTAND

# *Your handicapped child*

The Tavistock Clinic, London, was founded in 1920, in order to meet the needs of people whose lives had been disrupted by the First World War. Today, it is still committed to understanding people's needs though, of course, times and people have changed. Now, as well as working with adults and adolescents, the Tavistock Clinic has a large department for children and families. This offers help to parents who are finding the challenging task of bringing up their children daunting and has, therefore, a wide experience of children of all ages. It is firmly committed to early intervention in the inevitable problems that arise as children grow up, and to the view that if difficulties are caught early enough, parents are the best people to help their children with them.

Professional Staff of the Clinic were, therefore, pleased to be able to contribute to this series of books to describe the ordinary development of children, to help in spotting the growing pains and to provide ways that parents might think about their children's growth.

## THE AUTHOR

**Valerie Sinason** is Consultant Psychotherapist in the Child & Family Department, Tavistock Clinic, London, and Psychotherapist Convenor of the Mental Handicap Workshop there. She is a highly regarded poet and writes regularly on mental health issues in *The Guardian*. She is author of *Mental Handicap and the Human Condition*. She is married with two children..

# UNDERSTANDING

# *Your handicapped child*

## *Valerie Sinason*

of

THE TAVISTOCK CLINIC
*Series Editor: Elsie Osborne*

## ROSENDALE PRESS

First published in Great Britain in 1993 by:
Rosendale Press Ltd
Premier House, 10 Greycoat Place
London SW1P 1SB

Design by Pep Reiff
Production Edward Allhusen
Typeset by Ace Filmsetting Ltd
Printed in the United Kingdom by Redwood Books

British Library Cataloguing in Publication Data
A catalogue record for this book is available from
The British Library

ISBN 1 872803 65 2

# CONTENTS

# A NOTE ON LANGUAGE

In every country the words used to describe physical and mental handicap change every few years. This makes it very difficult for parents, professionals and people with different kinds of disabilities and handicaps to know exactly what is being spoken about.

The title of this book includes the term "handicapped" as that is the most common internationally understood term. However the book also makes use of other descriptive terms such as "learning disability" (as an alternative to "mental handicap") and "physical disability" (as an alternative to "physical handicap"). The terms "Mild", "severe" and "profound" describe the severity of the handicap.

Many parents, professionals and people with disabilities have strong views about which term they prefer. In a personal meeting it would be a matter of ordinary courtesy to check the preferred term. In writing a book something more standardised is needed. I am therefore sorry for any offence caused by the terms I use in this book. However, I do think we need to be aware that the very speed with which names and terms get changed is a problem. It shows the difficulty we have in dealing with this issue.

# INTRODUCTION

Your handicapped child is first and foremost your child; a child with the hopes, fears and problems of other children as well as his or her own unique personality. In 1993 in many countries in the world your child has even more possibilities than previously. There is a greater awareness of the potential in each individual, regardless of the severity of their physical and/or mental handicap or learning disability. Families, schools, hospitals and residential homes are more aware of children's emotional needs as well as their medical and educational ones.

Children and adults with disabilities are also living longer and, in some countries, pioneering programmes in the community or the transformation of hospitals into villages, are providing enriching environments for life. This helps with a major fear many parents with severely disabled children have – namely – who will look after my child when I am unable to? Although all parents worry about what will happen to their children when they are old or after they have died there is a difference when your child has a serious disability.

Planning for the future gives all the family greater confidence, especially when a member needs the extra or continuous help and support of others in order to live. However, planning is an enjoyable and necessary part of parenthood with all children. Planning for the future is not just a matter of practical issues – there is an emotional preparation that has to be achieved too. Parental hopes for children are part of this.

"My older daughter came into the world easily and she has gone through the education system easily too. My younger one has cerebral palsy and had physical difficulties and mental ones too from birth. Our plans for our older daughter included primary and secondary school choices and even university – and she has now graduated. Our plans for our younger one included speech therapy and physiotherapy as well as the best special schooling we could find. We wanted both of them to fulfil their potential. Joan, our oldest, gained an upper second in History at University this year and Julie, after years of shyness about her speech defect, gave a public talk at her Training Centre. Those two events crowned our year."

Peter and Leonie's hopes for their daughter were different as Lynette was multiply handicapped. She had no verbal speech, sight or hearing and would never have use of her legs. "Touch and smell are her only senses that work and we wanted to make sure that we could offer her the best environment to develop that." Due to their fund-raising attempts with other parents of children at the same school Lynette has enjoyed a special unit modelled on the Dutch "Snoezelen" which offers changes in heat, smell and tactile experiences. "Seeing her in the special safety harness that allows her to be in the jacuzzi and watching her put her fingers in the water and smile gave us as much pleasure as our son scoring a goal in his school's football finals."

Parents have hopes and plans for each child, that, on the whole, are properly suited to them – whatever their difficulties and strengths. This book is to help you be in even more touch with your own child's unique problems and potential.

If you have a child with a handicap or disability, this book is intended to strengthen your ability to deal with the emotional experiences involved. You are not alone, however much it feels like that. Not being average, not being in the majority, whether due to race, religion, class, economic or educational position, physical or mental handicap can make people feel very isolated. However, just within the United Kingdom nearly six and a half million children and adults have some kind of disability. Within the United Kingdom there are 360,000 children born with disabilities. In the world, over 1% of all new babies born will have some kind of disability. When we add to that figure the families and friends and professionals in contact with those millions of adults and children we can see what a powerful group we are part of in changing attitudes and provision.

Nearly every major organisation for people with different disabilities was started by parents. Parents who join up with other parents with the aim of aiding their children's independent development form a major political lobbying group as well. As parents, professionals and people with disabilities have joined together more effectively to show the need for better services the last few years have witnessed a major new development. There are now an increasingly large number of organisations run by disabled people. These include "People First", a self-advocacy organisation of and for people with learning disabilities, The Association of Disabled Professionals, the Association of Blind and Partially Sighted Teachers and Students and the British Deaf Association.

It makes a big difference to children with disabilities, and their parents, to have such adult role models. One mother commented "When I went to see Margaret Kennedy, of Keep Deaf Children Safe, with my daughter, it had a huge impact on both of us to realise that Margaret herself was deaf. Seeing her move from signing with my daughter to talking to me gave my daughter a sense of how it would be possible to be bi-lingual and have a professional position. I think that was even more important to us than the problem we had gone to her for."

In Sweden, Germany and England children with Down's syndrome, cerebral palsy and learning disabilities have had the opportunity to go to cafes with their parents where the cooks, waiters and waitresses have all got learning disabilities. In the village and hospital in Neuakerode, Germany where Dr Christian Gaedt is the Medical Director, the shoemaker has a learning disability and so have the workers in the highly profitable bird-breeding enterprise.

In other words, good provision, high expectancy and a working partnership with parents, professionals and the child minimise the impact of the disability and maximise the individual potential.

In the Tavistock Clinic Mental Handicap Workshop we make a division between the different kinds of intelligence an individual possesses. However difficult it might be for an individual to manage certain academic tasks like basic reading, writing, arithmetic or logical thinking, he or she might have a large capacity for "emotional intelligence". By that, I mean an ability to make relationships and understand personal feelings. However handicapped an individual is by brain-damage, chromosomal abnormality, illness or environmental trauma an ability to make sense of the environment and develop a capacity for love, hope and emotional development can be there intact.

"More than anything else, I wanted to love someone and get married. I wanted to get married and I wanted a job and a home. And I got them," said Maureen, aged 26. Those words express a sentiment many young people feel. There is nothing unusual about them. However, Maureen had a severe learning disability. Her husband had a mild learning disability. They met at a local club and went out for two years before they got married. Maureen and her husband both have jobs stacking supermarket shelves. Despite a high level of unemployment they have proved to be reliable employees. The only concession to their disability is that Maureen's social worker helped to find suitable council accommodation and visits regularly to offer help with the paperwork for gas and electricity bills.

Maureen's school for children with severe learning disabilities did not offer any sex education or classes in parent-craft or relationship-building. However, her parents' recognition of her personal worth and her own unique qualities combined to allow her to grow into an adult who could achieve her aims.

Here are some words from John, aged seventeen, a young man with cerebral palsy and a mild learning disability.

"I wanted to go out in my wheelchair by myself. Into the shops and into the park. I wanted to choose when I went out instead of waiting for someone who was free to take me. I was very scared of whether I would remember where there were safe places to cross. I worried about falling out of my chair or a car knocking into me. I worried nobody would see me behind the shop counter because I was too low down or that they would not understand what I said because of my speech defect. But I did it. I went out for twenty minutes. My arms ached because I haven't got an electric chair. But I went into the lift – pressed the button, went down and out into the street, across the road and into a supermarket."

John's aim was just within his reach. In the last block of flats his family lived in he would not have been able to accomplish his courageous aims for independence. An architect, without training in the needs of disabled people, had made the lift buttons too high for someone in a wheelchair to reach. A good family GP and social worker joined forces to help the family move and John's own abilities ensured he made good use of it. The local authority then realised they needed to include architectural features that would aid disabled people in all new plans.

Maureen's and John's successful accomplishment of their aims is a reminder to new parents that a diagnosis of disability does not mean that the possibilities of a fulfilled life are destroyed. Indeed, some parents comment that the personality of their disabled child can sometimes bring them more pleasure than the personalities of other people in the family.

However, in order to properly appreciate what is strong and hopeful most parents need the chance to be allowed to express their sadness that a child has been born with a disability.

There is a difference between having an intact mind and a severely disabled body and having a severe learning disability and an able body. Having both severe mental and physical handicaps, like Lynette, means holding onto different aims and aspirations. This book will not be able to single out every kind of disability. However, there are important shared features and shared questions. How do we communicate with a child who can't talk? How do we provide the best environment? How do we think about change and development when there aren't normal milestones? What does it feel like to know you are different?

CHAPTER ONE

# PREGNANCY AND FEAR OF DISABILITY

The psychoanalyst Donald Winnicott once said there was no such thing as a baby - only a mother and a baby. Without a primary caregiver a baby would not be able to survive. Where a baby has a disability this is even more true. For parents to have the necessary emotional space to understand their baby and his or her development they have first to understand the impact of the handicap on themselves. After that, they are dealing with the usual ups and downs of family life. All the books in this series are relevant for parents with handicapped children and can be read in conjunction with this book. Where this book is different is in highlighting the particular emotional and environmental difficulties that can occur when there is a handicap.

At an exercise class for pregnant women , one young mother-to-be, Anna, proudly announced that her husband's parents had bought her a magnificent pram. After praising its colour, shape and useful features she hastily added "I don't want it delivered to my house yet." "Why not?" asked a friend. "Just in case," replied the woman emphatically. There was no reply. That brief coded message was clearly understood. The pram was for a real living baby. Until the baby was born such a present was seen as premature. Indeed, it could even be irrationally seen as a dangerous present.

Such a conversation can be heard all over the developed world. The process of pregnancy is not certain. Miscarriage in the early months, or a spontaneous abortion later on, are possible despite medical advances. There is a magical fear in some couples that if they show how much they are longing for their baby to arrive they will cause its death.

The possible death of an unborn baby is difficult to speak about. "Now that I am past my third month it feels safer," says one pregnant woman. The baby is "it" – and is described in terms of chronology. Only rarely are such discussions more open.

Even more taboo than thinking and talking about the death of an unborn baby, is thinking and talking about a baby with a handicap or disability. Not many parents-to-be lie awake hoping their child will be born with a disability. However loving, inspiring or gifted their child turns out to be and however strong the bonding and the pleasure, it needs to be acknowledged that very few parents anticipate the possibility with pleasure.

When a man and woman hope for a baby, they hope that their baby will be at least as intelligent and fit as they are. However much we strive to include different degrees of difference in our concepts of what is normal, we never fully succeed. For most parents initially, a baby born with a disability – especially a mental or multiple one – something has gone wrong. I emphasise the word "initially" because in many families, after the initial shock is worked through, the child is the proper part of the family that a child needs to be. "It makes me feel really embarrassed now to remember how I felt when Zoe was born," says Kay whose daughter Zoe was born with Down's syndrome. "Now she is just Zoe. She has good days and bad days. She can be rude or loving. But then she was 'it'."

I am mentioning these painful issues at the start of the book because if they are not given a proper place none of the ordinary pleasures and stresses of parenthood can be thought about.

# "If all goes well"

"If all goes well," said Mary, "the baby will have my study as her room and then when she is 2 she will go to the little nursery round the corner."

"If all goes well" is often the hopeful phrase that hides all the different possibilities of disability and handicap. Parents need to fantasise and anticipate the future. We imagine years ahead. So long as these fantasies do not become fixed patterns of expectancy they can help us grow into our role. When we imagine how our child will look, how intelligent he will be, what kind of schooling and relationships he will have, we are carrying out a parental task in enjoying anticipating those stages and thereby preparing for them. In such fantasies very few parents would imagine a child in a wheelchair, a blind child, a toddler with a profound learning disability, an autistic adolescent, a profoundly disabled adult child who cannot feed, wash or dress himself.

# "Don't mention the subject"

Joan was unusual. "Every month of my pregnancy I would look in a medical book to find out what complications there could be at each stage of my pregnancy. I wanted to be prepared for whatever baby I had. I found myself watching handicapped children in the park or in the street." At her antenatal class she found other mothers-to-be turned away if she tried to bring up questions about the possibility of handicapped babies. "I was told by one friend that mentioning the subject depressed everyone and that could affect the babies they were carrying." We are back to the same kind of magical thinking that made Anna not want her pram until her baby was safely delivered.

# Preparing for disability

However, women prepare themselves for the birth of their babies and the possibility of handicap in very different ways. Janet was thirty-five when she gave birth to a baby daughter, Linda, with Down's syndrome. "I avoided thinking about the possibility of handicap throughout my pregnancy. My doctor wanted me to be screened because of my age. However, I could not manage to go through with that screening because that meant thinking more seriously about the possibility of handicap. No-one in my family or friendship circle had ever had a handicapped baby and I could not imagine it and did not want to." Once Linda was born Janet suffered acutely for the first three weeks but was then amazed at the strength of their bonding. "Linda is nineteen now. She can read, write and cook. She is a good judge of character and I have every hope she will eventually marry."

Janet thinks she did not prepare herself for having a handicapped baby. However, in choosing not to be screened, perhaps she had unconsciously made a choice to keep her baby regardless of its possible handicap.

Some women know that they or their partners have the inner resources to manage whatever problems their unborn baby will provide them with. Others equally know that they will not manage. Different countries offer very differing levels of provision and support to families with a handicapped child. Agneta, in Sweden, was not prepared for having a baby with a disability. However, early counselling, extra financial aid and excellent support services made a huge difference. Pauline, in an inner London Borough, was also not prepared for a disabled baby. There was no counselling or financial aid. There was also no special needs nursery. The good support provided over the baby's physical developmental needs was not enough to make up for the other deficits and Pauline gave up her baby for adoption.

# The chance factor

Mary was nineteen years old, single and pregnant from a drunken encounter at a party. Her baby, Sarah, was born nine months later – perfectly normal. Nora was twenty-six years old, married and pregnant at a time she and her husband had chosen. Her baby, Steven, was born with a rare chromosomal abnormality. Sandra, married, aged forty, had tried to get pregnant for over twenty years. She never succeeded. When young girls dream of when they will have a baby they rarely consider the possibility of being infertile, unthinkingly pregnant or having a baby with a disability. The idea that such issues are to a certain measure out of control is extremely painful.

Whilst there are some guidelines to ensure the safest possible pregnancy, it is very rare to be sure of the outcome. We know that malnutrition and poor diet in the expectant mother adds to birth complications for the baby. We also know that babies of mothers under twenty and over thirty-five are more likely to experience difficulties. Smoking and drug-taking, syphilis, rubella, diabetes and high anxiety can also have an impact. Some conditions – like fragile X – can be transmitted genetically whilst others, like Down's syndrome, are more likely in babies whose mothers were over thirty-five. In fact, over half of all babies with Down's syndrome in Europe are born to mothers over thirty-five.

However, many babies with disabilities or babies who

will acquire disabilities are born each day to couples who are healthy, maintain the right diet and are the optimum age. It is estimated that 1% of the new babies born in the world each year will have a physical or mental disability or handicap. An estimated million babies world-wide will be born with Down's syndrome alone.

# Creating support

Some mothers, facing poor or inadequate support and services, find the inner resources to create a new service themselves. Nehama Baum, for example, an Israeli social worker, gave birth to a son, Muki, with cerebral palsy and deafness. She gave up her work to teach Muki. "Right from the start, he had no control over any part of his body. I taught him how to use his hands, how to hold his head, sit, stand and walk. I also insisted on him being integrated into a toddler group." In 1976 the family moved from Israel to Canada and Nehama started an Institute to help such multiply handicapped children like her son. As an adult Muki is now able to use database, word processing and spreadsheet software and has a computer post in his mother's organisation which is named after him.

Many of the major organisations dealing with disabilities were started by parents.

# Premature birth, abortion and disability

In January 1993 the Office of Health Economics produced a report "Born too Soon" on those very premature babies who are profoundly handicapped for life. One in five of every premature baby suffers some kind of neurological impairment and the report questioned the "almost experimenting" decisions of doctors in looking after babies of only one pound (500 grams). Whilst in 1980 at the Hammersmith Hospital in London only two babies survived out of eight who were born

19

between 26 and 27 weeks, by 1991 56% survived.

There are ethical and economic questions involved and, of course, some people question whether even considering economic factors is ethical. Neonatal intensive care for babies weighing less than 3 1b 4 oz costs millions of pounds a year in the UK. Such babies are 50% more likely to need special schooling. Whilst governments have to deal with the economic priorities, parents and doctors face other dilemmas. It is easy to condemn expensive medical interventions when it is not your own family who might benefit from it. It can also be difficult to acknowledge that many of us owe our own lives and health to research that was condemned as impractical.

The Johnsons praise the hospital that helped their baby survive. Benny had weighed only one and a half pounds. "I was just like a bag of sugar," he said to me. Although he spent the first few months of his life in an incubator his parents stayed with him and his sensitive medical team provided lambswool for him to lie on. Although it was clear he had a severe mental and physical handicap his parents and the medical team all felt proud of his spirit to survive and their shared endeavour to help him live.

Once they were able to take him home the situation was very different. "We felt part of a family in the hospital. Everyone was sharing in Benny's struggles to live and thrive. We were supported round the clock. Once we got home it was very different. I was even told it was selfish of me to want him to live given he was so handicapped and that I was burdening the state by asking for extra help."

Parents can be made to feel selfish for wanting their baby to survive or for not wanting their baby to survive. David and his wife did not have a choice. They were only in their mid 20s when their multiply disabled daughter was born.

They were at an optimum age for healthy child-bearing and did not have any test. At a group for parents with handicapped children David commented – "To be honest – even though I love my daughter now – if we'd have known she had Down's syndrome my wife would have had an abortion."

For mothers who had rubella during their pregnancy and did not choose to have an abortion or who live in a country where an abortion is illegal, this discussion is extremely painful. It is also extremely painful if you are a child or adult with a mental or physical disability.

Emma, a young woman with Down's syndrome, commented "It makes me sad when I hear on TV or on the radio how there are tests to stop people like me being born. People think I do not understand because I have a mental handicap. But I do." Flora, a young woman university graduate with severe physical disabilities commented – "Those words 'screening' for 'problems' in the unborn baby. I can not stand them. It is me and people like me they are screening against."

"Screening", when it is linked to abortion, rouses very powerful feelings. The attitude to abortion varies in different countries. Since 1967 in the United Kingdom an abortion is legally allowed if two doctors consider continuation of the pregnancy would involve risk to the life of the woman, risk of injury to her mental or physical health, risk to her family or if there was a substantial risk that the child would be seriously physically or mentally handicapped.

Different countries and religions have very strong and differing views on abortion. Even within a single country there exists a wide range of opinions. Jean's son had cystic fibrosis. "When I hear of people having abortions because they know their baby is handicapped I cannot bear it. At times I feel deeply jealous that they are not having to suffer like me

21

and at other times I am sorry for them because you pay a price for denying life as well as for dealing with its damages."

Pregnancy, the creation of life and the termination of life are powerful processes. Right from the start, two people have joined hopefully together and something has happened that is not normal. This is difficult. However, by acknowledging the pain and distress real pleasure and love can be experienced. In the few situations where this is not possible alternative solutions can be considered.

# CHAPTER TWO

# YOUR HANDICAPPED BABY

## A public event

There you are with your new baby handed to you. You are, if you are lucky, surrounded with cards, flowers and presents. In your home there will be a carry-cot or crib waiting expectantly for the new occupant. There may or may not be an older child struggling with jealousy. There are likely to be relatives and friends who are waiting to meet the new arrival.

Giving birth to a baby is a very public moment. Even in difficult times, the birth of a baby is something that brings hope and pleasure. The human race would die out if we did not view birth as a major life event.

Since there is such a communal pleasure when a healthy new baby is born it is also not surprising that when the baby is born distressed, in pain, or with a disability, the family experience more difficult feelings. There can be shame, guilt, fear, pity, anger, revulsion as well as love. It is not just the family who experience these difficult feelings. The medical staff can add to the family's distress when they have not been trained and supported to understand their own sense of shock.

One mother's account, that I reproduce here with her permission, has been the experience of hundreds. "The nurse told me I had a daughter quite nervously. She did not say 'You have got a lovely daughter.' She handed her to me quite quickly. The doctor did not want to spend long with me either. When my husband and I looked at our baby I suppose we looked at her rather quickly and brusquely the way the nurse looked at us. I can't forgive myself now. She is such a lovely daughter."

Until all medical and nursing schools offer training in how to break such news to parents and how to explain the diagnosis as clearly as possible, parents are likely to have their own shock magnified.

"I will never forget what the Doctor said to me. There I was with my new baby in the crib by my side in a crowded ward. He cleared his throat nervously and very quickly said that my baby had severe handicaps, that he would never be able to do anything independently and perhaps I should give him up for adoption or send him away to a boarding school as quickly as possible and start on another pregnancy." That mother never forgot her sense of public shame at being spoken to in that way in the ward. Her son is now twenty-three and living independently in a group home.

Whilst it is rarer now for medical staff in the UK to advise a parent to "forget" their baby at birth, in countries with poorer provision it is common. Dr John Tsiantis, a pioneering child psychiatrist in Greece, has been working hard to ensure proper provision for handicapped babies and their families so that the tragedies of Leros are not repeated. Leros is an island colony for mentally handicapped people in Greece which stands as a symbol of the results of poor provision for handicapped children. "Forgetting" the existence of a handicapped child means depending on the kindness of untrained, poorly paid, badly treated staff in under-equipped primitive conditions. Every country in the world has a Leros.

I am not talking here about parents who decide it is in the best interest of their child to send them to a good boarding school. Where a parent, even with support, is not able to bring up their child, allowing others to try whether through schooling, fostering or adoption, can be the most helpful act and I discuss this later.

How should doctors and nurses speak to parents about their child's diagnosis? The Pattersons were devastated when they saw the physical defects of their baby (now aged 5). However, in the midst of their shock they could take in what the sympathetic Doctor said. "On his ward round he asked if we would like to come and see him in private. He checked when the baby's next feed was so it wouldn't interfere," said John Patterson. "He offered my wife the most comfortable chair as she was holding the baby. He said we must have got a surprise when we first saw the baby. He told us what was wrong with it and what that meant. He said he knew we had got a shock and all parents did at first. It was natural. He told us Timmy would never have a normal life but no-one knew what his real potential could be because he was only just born and everyone had something unique in them. He asked if we wanted him to explain the diagnosis to my mother – who was very worried – and he said we could come back and speak to him as soon as it had sunk in."

John Patterson had first seen his baby as an "it" – not a person with a name. However, in recounting the Doctor's sympathetic approach "it" slowly turns into "Timmy" and we can see how the response of the Doctor has helped the parents acclimatise.

Professor Sheila Hollins of St Georges Hospital, London has developed a way of ensuring that the medical students she trains will be sympathetic doctors when dealing with babies with learning disabilities (mental handicap). "All medical students as part of their training have to learn to work with people with learning disabilities. When they come to me I arrange that their first half-day event will be a drama workshop. This is organised by a drama group who all have learning disabilities. Having an enjoyable experience like this changes their sense of values about disability. In addition, each student is asked to observe the lifestyle of someone with a learning disability in their own home and ask them a list of questions about their likes and dislikes. This allows students to see what a good quality of life is possible when previously they had only understood disability as something that should be screened for and terminated."

## "I knew something was wrong"

As well as being concerned when doctors do not tell parents sensitively and privately a full diagnosis and prognosis, there can also be extreme anxiety when parents sense something is wrong that the doctors are not aware of.

Sometimes it is immediately visually noticeable that a baby has a handicap or is ill. Other times, a parent can pick up a sense that something is wrong before there is medical proof. Ruth was born four weeks premature. The doctors were satisfied by her progress but her mother was not. "I knew there was something wrong with her the moment I held her," said her mother. "Nobody listened to me. They just thought I was depressed. One doctor told me it was because I had ambivalent feelings to her that I thought there was something wrong. I am sure I did have mixed feelings about her – don't all parents? But I knew there was something different – something wrong – and it took them nearly a year to find it."

It is very difficult for parents to realise that not every condition is diagnosable at birth. Sometimes it is not that a nervous doctor is withholding difficult information but that there is no clear sign. However, the way any professional speaks to parents at such vulnerable moments aids or hinders their ability to parent. One doctor has found it helpful to say "If you think something is wrong that is important we will have to keep a regular eye on it. However, at the moment, nothing is showing on the tests we can do."

When a baby is born with a disability the process of being born and entering the outside world can be complex and uncomfortable. Sometimes major medical interventions are needed to ensure the baby's survival. Sometimes, the baby has to stay in intensive care for several weeks. Illness, pain or discomfort can make feeding and sleeping more difficult. The very moments that usually help mother and baby to become closer can themselves be the most unbearable.

"He was tiny – just a red scraggy bundle," said Irene. "He wouldn't stop crying. When I tried putting him to the breast to comfort him – which always worked with my other kids – he just screamed all the more. Nothing I did seemed to be right and we all got more and more exhausted. He couldn't sleep and he couldn't feed and he wasn't comfortable – whatever position you put him in." Later, she sadly commented that her family had stopped visiting as they found it depressing.

## Shame

A more common, though less spoken about feeling, is shame, both personal and familial. One mother, Anita, told me – "I felt shamed before my family. They wanted me to have a fine boy and I had produced a boy just as they wanted – but he had cerebral palsy." She also worried that the existence of a

27

handicapped child in the family would spoil the marriage prospects of her daughter, although she was normal. Such fears and worries may be expressed in many different ways, according to cultural and other differences and expectations.

There are often difficult feelings of shame to deal with between the marital partners. A baby is a joint product and each partner hopes that the best of them will go into the recipe. When the baby comes out with any damage the partners can initially feel humiliated by the fantasy that something damaged or damaging in them has been passed on. If these feelings are not shared and thought about it can lead to further stress on the relationship.

It is very frequent in ordinary family arguments for a parent to say "Your daughter is being naughty" or "your son won't do as he is told". When fraught, many parents temporarily try and genetically disown the source of aggravation! Where the child has a permanent irreparable disability this genetic disowning takes on a more serious quality.

Where there is a disability that is strongly noticeable at birth parents get a shock at first, but then, if all goes well, they recover. Babies are amazingly resilient. What is harder for the baby and the parents is if the shock does not go away. A mother's eyes are the baby's first mirror. As babies, we all need that mirror to say that we are the fairest of them all – that we are the most beautiful baby in the world. Where parents are depressed or feel guilty about the handicap the baby can look up into depressed eyes and take in an image of himself as someone depressing. Where the parent takes a long time to recover, the baby or toddler takes a long time to trust there could be anything worthwhile in them.

However, it is important to remember that it not just babies with a disability who can meet this response. Babies who are born into a family that is not prepared for them, or to parents who actively do not want them, babies who are born to a parent at a time when they are deeply depressed because of different life events, babies born at a time of marriage break-up or after the death of someone in the family – all these can face an initial depressed environment. All these babies can also be in an environment that improves.

Mary was born unexpectedly, a late unwanted baby to her parents Tom and Sarah. From before she was born Sarah knew something was wrong. "I was sure something happened in the last stages of labour." Sarah was frightened to look at her. "I felt a bit bad I had carried her through to term not wanting her. I worried she could have gone wrong inside because I did not want her anyway. Then when my labour didn't go properly it was even worse. When I did look at her I didn't feel any real love. It was more of a – "Well – we couldn't help it – somehow you are here so we have to manage."

Sarah did not really manage though. She had a postnatal depression and Tom changed his job so he could be at home more. "We both felt angry with Mary for coming when we did not expect her and for coming out odd. I think it took us several months to begin to really care for her."

Sarah had gone to visit some friends with babies when Mary was 10 weeks old. All the other babies were smiling at their mothers and their mothers were beaming back. Sarah suddenly noticed, in a way she had never realised before, that Mary had never smiled and rarely looked directly at her. Looking at the happy other babies and the unsettled Mary made her realise how depressed she and Mary were. "In that one moment I suddenly was aware of a burst of love for Mary. I gave her a big hug and told her I loved her. She had her head turned away but as I continued to speak she looked at me with enormous surprise. It felt like the first time we had ever really

29

looked at each other. One week later she began to smile."

There are some babies who, because of the extent of their disabilities, take even longer to smile. However, many of the kinds of surveys that examine at what age a baby with a disability smiles do not look into how depressed the family are. When Sarah came out of her depression and felt attached to her baby, then Mary was able to make progress.

Sarah and Mary were able to bond after ten weeks with the help of Tom's support for his wife. Sometimes, attachment takes longer and sometimes it never gells.

## Strains on husband and wife

As I explained earlier, most parents at times wish they could genetically disown members of their family! In an average family, the children will bring pleasure to their parents as well as stresses. However, the moment the economic balance tips and the child brings too many anxieties or difficulties to the parents there can be a strain on the marital bond. It is not surprising to know that where a child has a severe disability there is a greater likelihood of parents breaking up. Often, it is the man who leaves, unable to bear the signs of what his potency has created.

Many couples do indeed stay together, but only too often the father retreats into his work or hobbies leaving his wife to deal with the day-to-day management of the child. "He bought a new car even though we were in difficulty financially. Whilst I fed the baby I could see him through the window polishing the car lovingly as if it was the proper baby, the brand new wonderful one. It broke my heart for him, for me and for our poor baby who must have known we weren't properly there for her at the beginning."

Some fathers, however, are able to be there physically and emotionally. One father, Graham, who worked with a disability service, made these comments to me. "I don't know why it should be, but Derek's handicap did not pose a major problem for me. Throughout my wife's pregnancy I had felt a developing bond with my pre-birth child and I knew I already loved that about-to-be baby whatever might go wrong. I could not take more than two weeks off to be at home after the birth but to make up for that I tend to take over from my wife when I get home. In my work I have been very aware of the way fathers tend to withdraw and leave everything to their wives. That makes it harder for the baby to develop. I want my son to be as independent as he can so I need to have plenty of time for him."

## Sexual strains

The birth of a handicapped baby often brings sexual problems to the fore. As it was an act of lovemaking that created the baby, there can be a primitive fear that lovemaking is in itself damaging. A parents' group often helps with these difficult feelings. When a woman is pregnant she can have many thoughts that she never shares with anyone. For example, "I wish I had got pregnant from the time we really made 'love' rather than that time. I was not really thinking loving thoughts then. I wonder if the baby knows that?" "Did it harm the baby that I cleaned the whole house out today?" "Did my husband shouting at me effect the baby?" "That black mark on the potato – did I eat any of it by mistake? Has it harmed the baby?" "Did the baby mind me having intercourse last night?" These kinds of thoughts are all forgotten when a normal baby is born. However, if a baby is born with a disability all those thoughts come back with a vengeance for both the mother and father.

# Another baby?

Parents can face difficult decisions over the completion of their family when they have a child with a disability. This can be particularly hard if the child with the disability is the firstborn. "I always wanted two children," said Mandy, "but when my first child was born with a handicap I did not think I would have the energy to go through that again. I know it is not likely to have two children with handicaps but I could not bear to risk it. Even if a second baby was normal I don't think I would have enough time for it."

Other parents find they manage best if they create a "normal" family around the handicapped member. "We wanted two children to begin with but after Kevin was born with cerebral palsy we decided to have a further two. We thought that if he was one of three the others would have shared support in having a normal sibling as well as help in dealing with a handicapped one."

Karen's first baby was a normal girl. Her second-born, a much-wanted son, had spina bifida. "We are not sure whether to have another one or stick with two which we had always planned. I don't know if it would be making Ian into a sandwich to surround him with a normal sibling at each end. Is that denial of the handicap?"

Some parents find it helpful to gain genetic counselling at this point.

# When it never gells

At the end of this book there is a list of organisations which offer help to parents and their handicapped children, but where specialist services like these or sympathetic GPs fail to help, sometimes a parent chooses to give their child up for adoption.

"I tried. I really tried," says Emma. "My daughter was

physically and mentally handicapped from birth and I knew I could not deal with it. My husband had left me. I was in a state and my finances were all difficult. But that wasn't the reason. I just knew I could not manage her. I rang social services and they were very sympathetic. I thought they would just tell me I was a cruel mother and should pull myself together – but they didn't. They knew I was frightened of hitting her if she cried more. And they linked up with a specialist agency who found a wonderful couple to bring up Emma. They have let me visit her even though they are now adopting her. I feel really good visiting Emma there as I know she is getting a better life than I could give her.

# CHAPTER THREE

# DAY TO DAY ISSUES

## Over-protection

When a toddler first tries to walk and falls over parents feel frightened and elated. Slowly they get used to the risks involved in ordinary development. However, when a child is born with a physical disability that feeling of protectiveness lasts longer. There can be a very difficult path to keep between protecting the child in the environment and denying a child the dignity of the normal risks of exploration. With some disabilities, the fear engendered in the parents is so great that they experience little pleasure in such physical stages. Four year old David had a mild learning disability and cerebral palsy. He would regularly have grand mal epileptic fits as well as minor "absences". His parents made him stay in his pushchair when they went shopping – even though he could walk – because they were scared of him falling over or having an epileptic fit on a hard surface. They had carpeted their home carefully, padding all sharp corners of furniture. It was indeed to their credit that David had not injured himself at home.

I saw David in a friendly child development clinic. This was a walk-in clinic for pre-school handicapped children. As well as a drinks and snacks machine for parents and accessible toilets there was a large play area. A multi-disciplinary team consisting of psychiatrist, paediatrician, child psychotherapist, occupational therapist, speech therapist and physiotherapist were all available informally whilst parents and children had a social context in which to meet.

Whilst other more handicapped children were busy with the large bright enticing toys or toddling to the different play areas there David sat very still on the chair next to his mother holding her hand. One of the toddlers on the floor suddenly fell over and started to cry. His mother quickly picked him up and comforted him and with a few moments he was off exploring again. However David sat transfixed in his chair. "It's all right" said his mother, "The boy is all right now." However David sat holding on grimly to ward off a sense of impending catastrophe.

When there was a chance to speak to David and his mother privately, it was noticeable the way David walked as if he were on ice. He held his mother's hand tightly and treated every piece of furniture along the way as a potential enemy.

Inside the room he leaned against his mother until she lifted him on her lap. He showed no curiosity in the room, the objects in it or me. It was quite clear that he had joined in with his family's crusade against physical danger. However, in a way they had not wished or expected, his youthful curiosity had become a victim of the crusade.

Once his parents were supported more and saw the way David's development was being stunted he slowly began to explore his environment and gain more pleasure.

# Ignoring the disability

On a sunny Saturday morning the Jenkins family went for a walk in the local park. They were a familiar sight locally in their matching tracksuits and much admired for their sporting abilities. Mr Jenkins jogged regularly and was a longstanding member of the local cricket club. Mrs Jenkins was a keen tennis player and had been a marathon runner before Marta was born. Marta had been named after a tennis champion even though a physical disability was evident at birth. Mrs Jenkins was determined not be a "martyr" about having a baby with a disability and did not want Marta to be a "martyr" to her disability either.

By following a strict regime of physiotherapy at home – and enlisting the help of friends and neighbours – Marta was able to walk and become physically co-ordinated beyond the wildest hopes of her doctors.

On this particular Saturday morning Marta, who was seven years old, was having difficulty keeping up with her parents. She would pull herself along for a few feet with great determination and then stumble and collapse. Her face would screw up and she would look about to cry but then her mother's call "come on Marta" would rally her strength again. As she passed a park bench she heard one elderly woman say to another "that's the handicapped little Jenkins girl. They've done wonders with her. No-one thought she would ever walk."

I was not watching Marta that particular morning. However many years later, the twenty-eight year old Marta was telling me about it. "I will never forget that moment because it helped me understand my parents. They were worried that if they made allowances for my physical difficulties they would be destroying my ability to lead a normal life. They hoped that by not mentioning my disability it would go away. This leaves me with mixed feelings. I know that if my parents had been too much in touch with my physical pain – and the walks and physiotherapy were like torture – I would never have been able to walk. On the other hand, their attempt to ignore my disability gave me a great deal of distress."

Many of the most capable adults with disabilities admit to this dilemma. They know that some of their talents are due to their parents' refusal to accept the disability. However, they also consider there was an emotional price to pay.

Carl knows that he can walk because his family and friends had rotas for manipulating his limbs. He had operations to lessen the impact of cerebral palsy on his legs as well as a spell of conductive education. "I have a friend who has never got out of her wheelchair. She has not seen or done half of what I have done. We both feel jealous of each other. She wishes her parents had helped her walk. I wish mine had let me rest."

Although this discussion is focussed on disability it could be about the difference in parental expectations in any home. More than one concert pianist has ruefully admitted that parental pressure to practise instead of going out to play was part of their background.

## Blaming the disability

At the other extreme, we enter the home of the Jacksons. They are a professional couple with a two year old boy, Ben, who has Down's syndrome, and a four year old girl, Sandra. Although the family home is a four-bedroomed house the Jacksons have kept the children in the same room "to help Ben be as normal as possible". Ben's main activity is knocking down his sister's toys and interrupting any activity she does not include him in. On this occasion Sarah has made a Lego

37

house. It is the most complicated structure she has built and she is very proud of it. Just as she puts the chimney on Ben toddles up to her and knocks it down – breaking some of the walls. Sarah bursts into tears and runs to her mother. "I hate Ben. He has spoiled my house. Keep him away from me."

Mrs Jackson looked at her daughter's outburst with surprise and disappointment. "Why Sandra, I'm surprised at you. Poor Ben has Down's syndrome so he can't do the same as you and he really wants to. Imagine what that feels like for him. You should never say you hate him. He can't help what he is doing. If you wanted to be a kind older sister you would make something with him."

It was not possible for Mrs Jackson to perceive that Ben might be a rivalrous two year old who wanted to destroy what his older sister could do. Nor did she consider it possible to protect her daughter from these attacks. Sandra had to share the burden of the handicap and the care of Ben. This failed to attend to either Ben's emotional needs or his sister's. Down's syndrome did not make Ben knock the house down – feeling jealous did – and not being in a setting where his jealousy could be thought about.

Marta's family ignored her disability and Ben's family over-emphasised his. In both these otherwise loving and hard-working families there was a difficulty in keeping to a middle path. "It is only now my father has got arthritis that he understands what physical pain is like," said Marta. "Now that he needs more physical attention he is willing to sympathise with me." Sandra grew up to become a residential worker in a Home for Adults with severe disabilities. Her childhood experience was clearly utilised by her. "If someone is rude I say they are being rude. I don't say – 'you poor thing it must be your cerebral palsy/epilepsy/down's syndrome that is making those horrid words come out of your mouth'."

# Brothers and sisters

Brothers and sisters of children and adults with disabilities rarely get the attention and support they need. One professional middle-aged man told me "I never got attention for myself as an individual. All the attention I got was related to Edward. I am known everywhere as the brother of Edward. In my village, at my work-place and in family and social gatherings my own personal identity is erased. It is very hard dealing with this now even though I am a married man with two children. It sounds defensive or rude to my brother if I point out that adults are not usually introduced in this way. It hurt me much more as a child. I did not want that position of dubious celebrity that is involved in being related to someone with a profound learning disability. If I did badly at school teachers told me I was becoming like Edward. If I did very well I was told I was compensating for Edward's difficulties. If I was angry with Edward my parents said I should feel sorry for him and if I ignored his violence to me I was told I was being a wimp. I hated him for years – not him as a person – but how his existence changed my life."

For twelve year old Sarah, there is a very different experience. "I was fed up being the only child and was really pleased when Mum said she was pregnant last year. When Beth was born she had lots of things wrong with her and she was tiny. We all thought she was very brave managing to survive and I loved her the moment I saw her. She is my only sister and I get very angry when friends at school think I must be upset."

Ben, a 17 year old has a different view. "When Danny was born with severe disabilities I really took to him and helped Mum and Dad as much as I could. It was fine at the beginning. But when it got to me studying for my exams there was little support for me. Danny would keep screaming for my attention and when I locked my bedroom door so I could study Mum said I was being unfair. I want to leave home in October to go away to University and I know Mum and Dad want me to go to a local university so I can help out. It is very hard. I really care about Danny and I want eventually to have a professional post within mental handicap services. I do admire Mum and Dad for the way they have fought for Danny. But I wish they could have had more space for me too."

With Ben and Sarah there was quite an age gap between them and their learning disabled siblings. What is the impact when siblings are closer together? Rivalry does seem to be more intense. Almost every child wants to be the cleverest, the strongest and the most attractive in the parents' eyes. It might be mistakenly assumed that children with a handicapped sibling would feel successful. However, children want to win in a fair race. Having a handicapped sibling means competitive ideas and wishes are very difficult to acknowledge openly.

Some children become emotionally disturbed, finding a way of becoming as needy as their siblings. Others find the pressure to be "good" and make up for parental disappointment overwhelming. Normal siblings can often end up joining the caring professions - like Sandra- or becoming a patient. Where parents have been well-supported by friends,family and professionals, it is easier for them to balance the needs of their children.

Julie and Ivan Boniface are the founders of "VOICE", a national organisation to offer support to families and adults with learning disabilities where abuse has occurred. They founded "VOICE" after successfully ensuring their daughter's abuser was taken to court. In being willing to spend so much time on these issues they have also been very concerned to provide fair attention to all their children. This means acknowledging the difficult times in family life openly. The family members have given permission for these comments to be published. They succinctly express some of the key issues thousands of families are experiencing.

### Gemma (sister) At 14 yrs.

"If only we could be a 'normal' family (whatever normal means) – so that we could go to a restaurant or shops without people making rude remarks about how difficult my sister is. They don't know she has a problem because she doesn't wear a badge saying "I am handicapped – I am different'. Sometimes I wish she could because then they wouldn't stare."

### Marc (brother) At 16 yrs.

"I cannot easily invite my friends to my home because they don't understand that a fully developed, what appears to be a normal girl – shows no sign of embarrassment by appearing nude when walking out of the bathroom. While my friends (male) look on in amazement and some humour, I feel stupid and ashamed for her, them and myself."

### Gemma (sister) At 7 yrs.

"My friends call her stupid and laugh and tease her, but I said it could have been you or your sister and you should feel sorry for her. I told them I don't want them to be my friends if they can be so awful and hurt my sister"

### Alex (brother) At 5 yrs.

"Nicole is special and different from Marc and Gemma and I love her because she is special."

Nicole herself commented "Why isn't my brain like yours and my sisters and brothers? It is sad, isn't it, that I am handicapped."

Where siblings and parents manage to mention these issues there is a chance for enriched development. Stephanie, aged twenty-two, is a medical student who intends to specialise in learning disability. "My youngest brother has Down's syndrome. Of course there were difficulties. There are difficulties with everyone in a family and with him there were more problems at times than anything else. However, my parents always acknowledged that and never expected us to bear it when he was being a particular burden. He is so much an important part of my life that I cannot imagine what it would be like without him and I want to help other families feel the same way."

## Toys and presents

One of the surprisingly difficult things early on is to find out which toys are suitable for your child's needs. Since new parents are often guided by the toymaker's assessment of what is age-appropriate there are many difficulties. Few toymakers have considered the needs of children with disabilities. "My next-door neighbour has been our best support," said 36 year old Susan whose daughter, Meg, was multiply handicapped. "But every birthday she becomes all embarrassed and either hands over a present clumsily or pretends she has forgotten it is Meg's birthday. It took me three birthdays in a row to understand what was happening and then I was able to speak to her about it."

Most toy shops do not carry specialist toys for handicapped children. Many of the toys that are suitable for children with disabilities can be spoiled by the fact that they state the "normal" age for use prominently on the covering. There is a difficult issue here because age-labelling is very helpful for the majority of parents and friends. We just need to be aware of how these generally helpful every-day issues can be experienced as painful by parents with learning disabled children. Susan's next door neighbour knew that nine year old Meg loved building bricks. She saw a colourful box of plastic ones and was going to buy them until she saw prominently displayed "Suitable for Under Fives" on the front. "Why did the manufacturers have to put an age on it? Surely it is only needed where a toy is physically dangerous?"

# Books

Another mother told me that the same problem existed when buying books. Seeing a colourful picture book with the statement "suitable for 7 year olds" depressed her as she knew it was for bright seven year olds and her twelve year old would not be able to read or understand it. "You can't go into a shop and say my twelve year old is like a six month old baby."

These experiences can highlight again the initial feeling of shame and failure. They remind the parent again of the difference between normal development and mental handicap.

At the age of twenty Nora came to see me with a child's picture book. She was proud that she could read it. "I know the words, don't I," she commented. I agreed. "It says this is for five year olds," she added uncertainly. "I am not five. I am twenty. I could not read this when I was five." I agreed and said it was very difficult. Some five year olds would be able to read the book but she couldn't when she was five. It was good that she could be pleased her reading had improved as well as important that she knew she was not a good reader. I added what a shame it was that so few books were written for adults like her; books about older things than a five year old would be able to understand but with easy words. Nora agreed.

With a blind child parents are faced all the time by the sense of loss they can experience when they see the beautiful bright colours of children's toys and their child cannot. Where there is a severe physical disability, parents can find sports departments particularly painful. "It was the football boots and tennis racquets I could not bear to go past" said one father. "Sports were my life in my teens and my early twenties and it hurts me each time I see all the sporting gear that my son could never make use of."

# Play

"However, if you do get beyond that to be excited when your child puts two bits of lego together, or laughs on knocking down a brick tower, you will be surprised at the amount of ordinary pleasure you can feel," says Professor Sheila Hollins of St. Georges Medical School, London. "The key issue is to know your child for who he really is not as who you would have liked him to be."

All children need play. Play is a serious way of exploring. Where a child has severe disabilities parents can be torn between a desire to educate and a desire to play. Six year old Cathy, a girl with a severe mental handicap, was enjoying some messy finger-painting. Her eyes were alight with pleasure as she plunged her fingers into the red and blue paint pots and plonked them onto the large white page. "Oh Cathy," remonstrated her mother, "show me how you are a clever big girl who knows how to draw a house." All Cathy's pleasure faded from her eyes. She tore up her picture and began to cry and rock. Within a few minutes a moment of play was transformed. This is not to say that there aren't times when a child needs to be directed from play to work. However, it is all too easy for a conscientious parent to be premature, and fail to allow their children such moments of pleasure.

"Other children had games and I had physiotherapy. Other children scribbled and made messes and I had social education training. Other children played kissing games in the cupboard and I had warnings about pregnancy. I never had play," is a common type of complaint.

# Sleep problems

Sleep problems are common for children with a mental handicap or physical disability. Muscle spasms, contractions, deformities, difficulty in moving can also make sleeping hard for those with a physical handicap.

Over half of all children with a mental handicap are estimated to have a serious sleep problem, involving waking their parents at least twice a week. More depressingly, sleep problems often continue as children get older whereas for normal children the stage is often passed through.

Stress in the family, sometimes caused by the strain of having a child with a handicap, can create an atmosphere where it is hard to relax and sleep. Some children with Down's syndrome, for example, can have respiratory problems. Children with epilepsy find it hard to settle. The reasons are likely to be emotional as well as physiological.

As parents you may find it helpful to make a firm but gentle boundary around bed time. In her book, "Through the Night", Dilys Daws discusses sleep problems in general and how they may be improved.

# Inappropriate sexual behaviour

Many referrals to clinics are made by schools and parents when there is concern about inappropriate sexual behaviour. This can include public masturbation, undressing, dressing inappropriately (a jumper and no clothes below the waist, for example). Practically every child in every culture learns in babyhood and toddlerhood that different parts of the body cause a different sensation. However, at a point when young children are able to follow adult cues about privacy some children with disabilities lag behind. Why is this?

Kelly, aged three gave up wearing nappies at night-time and became dry both day and night. She was extremely proud of herself. Having graduated from the potty to the toilet she suddenly became aware of her need for privacy and asked for the door to be shut. She no longer wanted to be undressed in public. Joseph, her older brother was five. He still wore nappies day and night and never used the potty. He was physically and mentally disabled. Whilst Kelly developed a sense of privacy around her new-found skill of being toilet-trained, Joseph became more and more public. Kelly could be seen jumping around doing what her mother called "a toilet dance" when she was worried she would not get to the toilet on time. Joseph would often pull his trousers down and urinate in public. It was suggested to the family that Joseph did not need an educational programme on privacy. On the contrary, it was precisely because he understood the meaning of privacy that he was now destroying it. His sense of shame that he could not manage to be continent was covered up by his "unashamed" exhibitionism.

Whilst Kelly could sometimes be observed pressing her vagina against the corner of a table her exploration of herself was carried out in private. Joseph, on the other hand, played with his penis in his infant class and when Kelly had friends over for tea. The family appreciated that this was not because he didn't understand the meaning of privacy.

Mandy, aged ten, suddenly started to masturbate regularly in her class for children with severe learning disabilities. Her teacher was worried at the possibility of sexual abuse. A meeting with her mother revealed that Mandy's older sister had just had a baby. "Mandy has been worrying if her body is normal like her sister's or whether there is something in her that would make any baby she had come out wrong." Some discussion on this with Mandy relieved her anxiety and her masturbation stopped.

Some children with profound learning disabilities may turn to their own bodies for comfort if there is no other stimulation for them. Sometimes sexually abused children masturbate in public, and so indirectly communicate what has happened to them. Whatever the reason, it is important to stress that it is not the handicap as such that leads to excessive masturbation.

# Mannerisms

Some children with severe learning disabilities have notice-able mannerisms that cause embarrassment to their families in public places. These are sometimes a real organic result of a disability (such as drooling from the mouth) or otherwise an exaggeration of a vulnerability (such as rocking, biting, hand-flapping and head-banging).

"I hate going on the bus with Jessica because everyone looks at us. She always has a horrid bit of dribble coming out of her mouth and I always wipe her mouth but the next bit is always faster than me. She rocks and moans and makes sudden silly jumpy movements that startle people." It is hardly surprising that people stare at such unusual behaviour. However, this kind of "negative celebrity" is very difficult to manage. It can make choices of holiday breaks even harder. "I wish there had been hotels for people like this instead of us always in self-catering so we wouldn't be embarrassed in a restaurant" is a common plea.

Although holiday schemes are rare there is at least one scheme for adults with a learning disability, started by Profes-sor Joan Bicknell of St Georges Hospital. It might also be worth while enquiring from one of the listed associations.

# CHAPTER FOUR

# SPECIFIC DISABILITIES

This section discusses some of the major disabilities in a little more detail. In some respects it may also be helpful for parents whose children suffer from some other disability.

## Blind babies and toddlers

Blind babies who are free of any other disability develop in the same way as other babies. "Susie smiled at me even though she could not see me. And she didn't smile when she was picked up by friends of mine. Her babbling was for me too." said her mother, Janice, proudly.

Janice helped Susie develop by encouraging her to explore her face with her hands. When she bent over Susie in her cot – after speaking – she would gently pick up Susie's hands and put them on her face. Touching games with toes and fingers also helped Susie get a sense of herself and her mother whilst father's beard proved a fascinating tactile experience. John would call Susie's name and place her hand on his beard. It was one of the ways he helped to develop her recognition of him. "I quickly found out that if I called Susie and moved my beard onto her hand it confused her because my beard wasn't where she heard my voice come from. So now I always call her first and she gets better and better at locating the sound and then she moves her hand towards it."

While the sighted baby enjoys reaching for a toy at five months, having eyes that can co-ordinate with his hands, the blind baby needs to develop ear–hand co-ordination. John had intuitively settled on the best technique. Shaking a bottle or rattle in front of your baby will encourage her to reach out to the sound. This does takes longer than for the sighted child but it happens. It also takes longer for the child with Down's syndrome.

The extra difficulty comes at a later stage. Blind toddlers experience more distress when their mother is not present as, unlike their sighted peers, they cannot hold a visual picture in their minds to help at moments of absence. If we think of the way sighted people like having photographs to help to keep absent or dead friends in mind – even though they have been able to create an internal image through visual contact – we can get some idea of the extra task a blind toddler has to achieve to make the first steps towards independence.

All toddlers fall over and find walking difficult. But the sighted toddler can see where steps are and visually learn to deal with cleaners, shoes or misplaced toys. The blind toddler will continue falling and has to learn about stairs and walls and pieces of furniture through a painful process of trial and error. One mother said "I could not bear Stevie falling over. Even though there was a soft carpet in the lounge and even though he was only a toddler, and all toddlers fall over I felt it every time he fell. I think I veered from being over-protective to being quite cruel and saying it did not matter. It did get better as he got older."

Parents have to learn to deal with these worries and provide their children with a realistic sense of independence. This can be aided if right from the start you provide comfortable floor space with no obstacles in the way. This means the baby and toddler have the chance to develop a sense of spatial security before teaching them the shapes of furniture and other objects. The floor provides a very basic sense of ground. Rocking games with mother or father on the floor, in which the baby or toddler is held but rocked at an incline help the child orientate to a falling angle.

# The blind child

The more that parents speak to their babies the more the babies learn to communicate. The blind toddler and little child can, if not disadvantaged in any other way, develop their language like any other child. However, some are only able to use their full range of vocabulary for what is actually near them. "Jane at four years could tell me that her doll had long straight hair with a silk ribbon on and she could tell me that her doll's dress was crumpled and needed ironing. But that was when she had her doll on her lap. It took me a long time to realise that her less talkative periods were when she was not in immediate reach of a range of objects that mattered," said her mother.

However, when Jane was five she amazed her father by managing to remember things he had forgotten. "She could remember every detail of our summer holiday even though it was months ago."

In the first five years parents are often concerned by two different features. Firstly, their baby has a more limited range of expressions because of not being able to see. This makes it all the more important to try and understand the baby's body communications. Secondly, at moments when a parent or a friend is not engaging the little child he can retreat into an empty state. "One moment James was smiling and chatting at me. Then, when I told him I had to concentrate on the cooking a moment, he was silent. When I turned round he was sitting rocking on the carpet. He went from being a handsome little boy to someone severely handicapped in seconds."

If we think of how dependent we are on sight for all our cues of daily living it helps us realise how talented our children are in finding other ways to communicate. It also, hopefully, gives us the chance to make the environment more helpful.

What can it feel like to have a spoon of food suddenly thrust in your mouth with no warning; to be picked up out of a cot, a pram or a chair with no warning, to trip over because someone has left one item of furniture in a slightly different position; to dare to walk to school with a "blind" stick only to find a car parked on the pavement, destroying the safety of the route? What is it like to not see whether someone is pleased to see you, neutral or cross?

Speaking gently and touching lightly before undertaking any physical action will aid your child's emotional and educational development.

Two mothers, Maureen and Donna were asked what was their biggest difficulty in bringing up a blind child. Maureen commented, "This may sound very strange – but it was over my cat. I have always loved cats but my last one – Snowy – would never settle on a lap to be stroked. She liked leaping round the room. I never minded when I watched television if suddenly she leaped onto my shoulder – even if I could not see her or did not expect it. However, my brave little Sarah who has ridden a bike and done all kinds of heroic things, just crumpled whenever Snowy landed on her. She could not bear not seeing when it was going to happen. I tried shutting Snowy in another room but that never worked. I know some friends with blind children who have pets – but it never worked with us."

Sarah eventually came to therapy for help in thinking about some aspects of her blindness. She selected a fluffy toy cat as her favourite therapy toy and threw it with great relish and accuracy at the therapist! Shortly after, she became less frightened of cats. Dealing with aggression is very difficult when you do not get visual cues.

Donna picked a different problem. "Daytime was fine. But Sam was terrified of going to sleep. He had terrible tantrums at bed-time and it took him a long time to explain that he was frightened by all the noises." During the day parents, friends or teachers explain the noises that can be heard and provide advance warning. Hoovers, water boiling, fat sizzling, taps dripping, a curtain flapping, the wind howling through a chimney – every home is full of noises that can be taken for granted if we are sighted.

At night-time no-one is there to explain every noise such as the creaking of stairs or the planes that pass overhead or the hums that can come from fridges and freezers, which are barely perceptible in the day when everyone is speaking. Stories at night-time and gentle discussions can help to settle the child. As I mentioned in the earlier section on sleep, many children with disabilities of all kinds have this problem, and there is often a combination of the child's vulnerability and the parent's worry.

# The blind child at school

Angela teaches blind children. What thoughts does she have for parents to think about? "One of the biggest difficulties I face is over how protective to be. It is fine when they are each seated at a table and the only things that move are on the table. But when they start being brave, walking and running I have to fight an urge to call out warnings all the time. It must be even more difficult for parents.

There is something else I would like to say. It is about colours. If a child has never seen a colour the whole concept is very difficult to understand. Some colours do not matter so much but when we talk about a 'dark' night or putting the light on, for example, that is very hard for my class. One child asked if the classroom light could be put on. (It was already on). I asked why he wanted it on and he explained 'to stop the rain'.

He was a very intelligent boy but he did not know how to use such language as he did not have a visual image for it. Some parents work very hard teaching a child to say the right colours. A couple of children in my class, for example, can say the colours of everything they are wearing even though the colour itself means nothing to them. They are very proud but there is a difficult thin line between encouraging a child to know what sighted people know and denying the actual handicap."

# Sex education

Many children and adolescents with disabilities are deprived of a normal sex education. There is a strange idea that if they cannot see, hear, speak or walk they will not be sexual beings. John, aged 16, a highly intelligent young man who eventually went to university, commented "No-one told me anything about my body. I think they hoped that if I was blind I would not see I had a penis. If I end up working with blind teenagers I will make sure they are properly educated. It puts you emotionally and socially at risk to not understand how your body works." This problem is true for adolescents with learning disabilities too.

# Deaf babies

Like blind babies, so long as deaf babies are not disadvantaged in other ways and so long as alternative ways of communicating are found the child can develop like any other. The development of emotional attachments are not affected by deafness and, as the deaf child has the benefit of sight, physical achievements are normal. It is in the sphere of language that more work is needed. In some countries there has been an extra handicapping process at work in that some deaf children have been deprived of sign language. Just as a blind child needs to develop ear-hand co-ordination to by-pass hand-eye, a deaf child needs hand-language to make up for difficulties in mouth-language. Sign language is a proper language in its own right and if taught from the start together with lip-reading avoids the risks of educational failure.

For a long time, because of a lack of professionals and parents who have learned sign language, deaf people were mistakenly thought to be mentally handicapped. The suppression of sign language led to the majority of deaf people having unintelligible speech.

It is hard to believe that all over West Europe and the USA until relatively recently sign language was actively suppressed. Out of approximately 8 million people in Britain with hearing disabilities only 55,000 have British Sign Language. Unlike many other disabilities, activists in this group recommend separate schools so that deaf children can have their own language as a first language.

# Down's syndrome

As with cerebral palsy there is a range of levels of disability with Down's syndrome. As well as learning disability, which can range from mild to profound, there is also a risk of congenital heart disease, hearing problems and severe chest infections. After the age of forty there is a higher than average risk of Alzheimer's disease. However, just a few decades ago an individual with Down's syndrome was barely likely to reach thirty years and now fifty to sixty is the average.

In babyhood, poor muscle tone and control and a larger than average tongue contribute to feeding difficulties and speech problems, although there has been a great improvement in language development.

All parents help their child's speech development by talking to them and playing with them. With Down's syndrome, additional games that help to deal with facial muscles and tongue control are helpful. However, as with all children with disabilities, parents have to be careful that play is still play and not physiotherapy!

An important myth to dispel with family, teachers and friends, is the idea that children with Down's syndrome are extra friendly. I have shown in my book "Mental Handicap and the Human Condition" that many children with Down's syndrome are encouraged to smile and hug people inappropriately. Whilst some individuals are more friendly than others, encouraging a child to fit a stereotype is not helpful.

One of the most important emotional issues to understand with a child with Down's syndrome is the impact of looking different. We nearly all underestimate the impact of this. A young girl told me "When I went on my school holiday I saw someone like me." In her integrated school there were a few children with physical disabilities but she was the only child with Down's syndrome. After the holiday she asked her mother for a mirror for her bedroom. She spent a long time examining her face. Eventually she was able to ask why she looked like the girl on holiday more than her own family.

In group work at the Tavistock Clinic we have found that it is painful for a child or young adult to be the only person with Down's syndrome in a group. A minimum of two is needed. Where parents are seeking ordinary schooling for their child they should check if there are other children with Down's syndrome.

# Autism

Autism affects around 11 children in every 10,000. Infantile autism starts before thirty months. These children have major problems in language and speech development and a special difficulty with pronouns, in understanding the use of "you", "I" or "me" for instance. They also lack ordinary response and eye contact with other people. They might have abnormal facial expressions and body postures, often with fixed, stereotyped body movements. A diagnosis of childhood autism will not usually be made until there have been three years of abnormal development. Eighty per cent of these children will be mentally handicapped.

What are the impacts on parents? Susan Reid, of the Tavistock Clinic Workshop specially concerned with autism, comments, "Parents whose autistic children look normal feel differently from the parents of noticeably disabled children. They often get singled out for criticism as bad parents when their children are perceived to be behaving oddly. This makes it harder to go out. Parents coming to the special workshop we run for them complain about the sometimes rigid diagnoses their children are given. Some are categorically told the autism is only caused by organic damage, often with the implication that nothing can be done. This puts them at the mercy of different professionals who either promise no cure or a complete cure. Our view is that there are multiple causes and we feel that, regardless of organic damage, therapy can assist emotional functioning. Many of the parents that I see are concerned about the impact of life's circumstances on their child and some find it hopeful to consider that if a factor in the origin of their child's condition is psychological there might be more possibility of change."

# Physical and other disabilities

A child with a physical disability who has no other disadvantage may be lucky enough still to have normal emotional development. However, the length of hospital stays needed, the degree of separation from their families, the amount of physical pain, all do have an effect, and make a special demand on a solid family base to overcome these difficulties. In many respects there are gradual improvements in the facilities for physically disabled children to lead a more normal life. For instance, more and more schools, colleges and universities are including ramps and suitable toilets, so that education, in particular higher education, is properly available.

The following is a summary of some other disabilities, with a brief note about each one. More help and information about many of these conditions may be obtained from the specialist associations listed at the end of the book.

CEREBRAL PALSY is a brain injury that results in movement difficulty. The primary lesion is in the brain and therefore irreparable, although in some cases surgery can improve an individual's physical functioning. Cerebral palsy can lead to severe mental handicap, epilepsy and speech defects, but this is on a continuum and some children have normal intelligence. Causes which are post natal include acute infantile hemiplegia, meningitis and encephalitis. Prematurity, anoxia, rubella or toxoplasmosis are also implicated in its causes.

ENCEPHALITIS is an infection affecting the brain substance. It can be caused by the same viruses that are connected with aseptic meningitis. It can lead to hemiplegia, paraplegia, epilepsy, emotional disturbance and mental handicap.

EPILEPSY. Grand Mal is the most common form, involving seizures with sudden loss of consciousness. Additional problems include possible injury from falling during a seizure and possible urinary and faecal incontinence. In the newborn child seizures can be recognised more by twitching or staring eyes, rather than convulsions, which in the first few days of life are usually due to birth trauma. Petit Mal is the name for brief, frequent lapses of consciousness but not associated with twitching or loss of balance.

Temporal Lobe Epilepsy can be heralded by fear, unpleasant smells, pain or tinnitus. There can be difficulty in speaking and hallucinations.

FRAGILE X Syndrome. Approximately one in every 600 males is affected by non specific mental retardation caused by a gene on the X chromosome. The fragile X is the most recognised and accounts for a large proportion of all mental handicap. It is usually severe and causes delay in speech and language. Regular features include large ears and a long face. One third of women carriers of the gene are themselves mentally handicapped. There are also male carriers of this Fragile X mutation who are intellectually normal. Their daughters will inherit the mutation but not be handicapped. However, their grandsons are at risk. All mothers of affected males and females are carriers. The recognition of these facts raises some ethical questions about identifying a boy who may eventually have affected grandsons.

The syndrome involves specific language problems too, including echolalia, stuttering and slurred speech, more so than with Down's syndrome. There is also handflapping and hand biting, poor eye contact and hyperactivity. At a major conference in the USA organised by Dr Randi Hagerman of the Denver Children's Hospital, it became apparent how relieved parents were to discover that their children's behaviour had some organic cause.

HYDROCEPHALUS is due to an excessive volume of cerebrospinal fluid and is associated with increased intracranial pressure and with mental handicap which may be severe.

NEONATAL ANOXIA  This is failure in the newborn

infant to breathe spontaneously immediately after delivery. Although the infant with severe anoxia might later show signs of mental handicap, cerebral palsy, epilepsy or behaviour disturbance, it is hard to say whether the infant was damaged by the anoxia or whether the anoxia could have been due to an underlying abnormality in the brain.

SICKLE CELL ANAEMIA is an inherited blood disorder that affects people of Afro–Caribbean origin especially, as well as some people from Asia and the Middle East. It can cause severe pain – especially with dehydration, at high altitudes, in pregnancy after exercise and stress. "I do not like white people", said a black 14 year old, "because when I was in school and in pain my teacher just thought I was playing up and did not listen to me and they sent me to psychiatry too. It was only there they found out I had sickle cell anaemia and there was nothing wrong with my mind. If white people got this I bet they would listen more."

SPASTICITY is one of the classifications of cerebral palsy. It can involve tetraplegia (in which all limbs are affected), paraplegia (in which mainly the legs are affected and not the arms) and triplegia (in which one arm is normal). Double hemiplegia is reserved for children with spastic tetraplegia in which the arms are more severely affected than the legs.

In some cases babies are affected by anoxia and birth trauma, other children are affected by disease and trauma in the first few years of life. Other classifications of cerebral palsy include athetosis, rigidity, ataxia, tremor and hypotonia.

SPINA BIFIDA is a bone defect linked with an abnormality in the spinal cord.

TOXOPLASMOSIS is an infection caused by a parasite which affects almost all animals. Women who catch this disease in pregnancy may have babies infected by it. This can cause hydrocephalus, brain lesions, severe learning disabilities, epilepsy and blindness.

59

# CHAPTER FIVE

# MEDICAL INTERVENTION

## Operations

Where a baby is born with a severe handicap or illness parents often face a double difficulty. At the same time as getting used to their new baby and all the difficulties he or she is in they are also being asked to give consent for operations. Tony commented, "We had only just taken in the severity of our baby's handicap. I was wishing he would die. When the doctor asked if he could operate I really struggled. I thought if I said 'no' then we would not have to deal with this problem. But I could not do that in the end. So Johnny had his operation and now he is eight and I am very grateful that life-saving surgery was available."

An operation raises all these worries and feelings in adults; but what is it like for the baby? There is an illusion that an operation carried out in babyhood does not hurt in the same way as later, as it won't be remembered. Whilst babies do not have a mental picture or concept of a hospital or operation, the intrusions into their body and mind are registered.

# Sensitivity

With various kinds of disabilities medical intervention is a regular experience. Whilst all doctors and nurses have received a good medical or nursing training, there are, of course, considerable individual differences in terms of their personal courtesy and sensitivity.

An Australian psychiatrist, Averil Earnshaw, watched the interaction between newborn babies and nurses in several hospitals. She noticed that rectal use of thermometers caused great distress in the babies whilst taking temperatures under their arms did not disturb them. The staff were not deliberately intruding unnecessarily on the babies, they had been taught to take temperatures that way and somehow that protected them from being in touch with the babies' distress. With help they were willing to change.

Whilst babies communicate their sensations by their body language, older children are able to tell us verbally. Twelve year old Naomi, who was born with cerebral palsy, comments, "I was left waiting in a cold room with a short smock on that did not cover me properly and I felt humiliated and ugly. When the doctor did come he never introduced himself properly. He just asked me to do different things with my legs that hurt me and then he spoke to the medical students about me."

John, who needed regular surgery, had a better experience at his hospital. "My doctor always came to say hello and ask how I was. He always explained what had to be done and why and he told me if it would hurt or not and how I was likely to feel after."

Sarah, who had a spinal deformity, had an unsuccessful operation that left her partially paralysed. "Why couldn't they all just leave me alone? I knew I could not walk properly. I accepted it. It was everyone else wanting me to look normal.

I am not normal. And now I am even less normal than I was."

# Cosmetic or necessary?

Sarah's comment raises a regular ethical dilemma. How much should a disability be accepted? Many operations carry a slight risk of failure. Sometimes, the danger of not having an operation is so severe, that the operation itself raises less anxiety. Sometimes, however, the operation is to ensure a cosmetic change.

"I kept having these operations. They hurt, hurt, hurt" said Martin, a fourteen year old with cerebral palsy and a mild mental handicap. "But I look better now because I don't walk so silly." This experience is unlike that of able-bodied adults who have waited years for cosmetic operations to deal with birth-mark blemishes and feel restored afterwards. They have usually thought about it a lot personally and the decision is their own.

Where a child, as opposed to an adult, is operated on, his or her own consent is less certain. Whilst Martin was pleased he didn't "walk so silly" after a painful series of operations, Mary was not. "I can't walk properly because of brain damage. People look at me because I can't walk properly. I go to hospital and it hurts. I can't walk at all for a long time. Then I still can't walk properly, just a bit less handicapped than before. But I am handicapped. Why couldn't my parents just like me how I was? Why do they have to try and change me and hurt me?"

Sometimes parents do try and change their children to make them as normal as possible because they cannot bear how different their children look. However, there are also parents who cope with their children's anger and hurt because they are sure that in the long run their child will have benefited from their decision.

"My body was tortured by doctors and physiothera-pists and then my parents making me do physical things all the time. But when I went back to see the first Consultant I had he was amazed. He had not thought I would ever be able to walk," said twenty-three year old Jeffrey.

Again, we can think this issue is only to do with disability. However, many parents have standards which they set for their children in the hope it will bring out their potential. Children, parents and doctors need to think very carefully about these issues together.

In Germany, for example, there was controversy over a new operation for Down's syndrome babies that would make their faces normal. Many parents were confused as to the ethical value of this. "If my child looked normal then he would get a response from strangers that is totally different. As he is he meets the world at its worst or best. He knows what to expect and so do others. If he looked normal he would get a friendlier instant response and then people would be confused that he was not normal," said one father. A couple whose baby had the operation had different views. "We can love our baby better now that we can look at her without always seeing how handicapped she is. It got in the way. We know she is handicapped but it helps us not having to see it all the time."

# CHAPTER SIX

# SCHOOL

When a child has a physical or a learning disability, or maybe both, many countries try to offer an extra educational input. In England, in partnership with parents and with the advice of a multi-disciplinary team, a Statement is made of the needs of the child if the school they are in does not seem to be offering suitable provision.

Although about 18% of all children have some special needs only 2% of all children "with severe and complex needs" are seen to be entitled to extra specialist support.

Although assessments are usually made at the request of the educational psychologist, or Head teacher, parents can request an assessment too. A full assessment is an expensive and time-consuming process. It takes at least a month for parents to hear if such an assessment will go ahead. If it does, all the professionals who work with the child make their reports and the parents make an important contribution. If the local authority decides to go ahead with a draft statement they show parents a copy and there is a period of time for changes to be made. A final statement is then made which parents can appeal against if they are not satisfied.

The statement of needs has to be reviewed every year by the local authority  and a second assessment has to be offered to children between twelve and a half and fourteen and a half.

More and more parents are seeking the help of the legal profession when they do not consider the Statement fair or when they do not think the local authority has properly implemented the Statement. Leading specialist lawyers carry about 150 cases relating to special needs.

It is now easier for parents to take legal action in England on behalf of their children as they can be helped with legal fees, a by-product of the 1989 Children's Act.

Tony had cerebral palsy and was severely mentally handicapped. His parents considered his speech his biggest problem. Tony was keen to communicate but no-one outside his immediate family could understand his voice. His statement of special needs supported that perception and underlined his need for speech therapy. Tony's area did not have any speech therapy time available so his desperate parents took the local authority to court in order to get him such treatment.

## Integration or segregation

In England almost 25% of all children with disabilities are educated in special schools compared to 7% in Italy and 5% in America. Every ten years or so the pendulum of opinion changes as to whether children with disabilities develop best in integrated schools or special schools. Most parents I have spoken to have the opinion that, politics aside, children do best in schools with high morale, good leadership and good relationship with parents. Sometimes a school claims to be integrated but the handicapped child is largely in a corner with an occasional support teacher and without gaining much attention whereas the local special school would have provided much more. Sometimes the special school has low morale and an ordinary school has a good Head teacher committed to making integration work. Parents know when their child is settled or not in the school environment. With any doubts, appointments should be sought with the class teacher initially and then the Head or an educational psychologist.

# The educational psychologist

I asked Dr Sheila Bichard, Consultant Educational and Clinical Psychologist and co-convener of the Tavistock Clinic Mental Handicap Workshop to describe the major role of the educational psychologist for children with physical or mental disabilities.

"Educational Psychologists are part of a team of professionals who are often called upon to assess the needs of children who may need special care and consideration in the schools. The EP tries to assess children, using cognitive tests. This assessment includes their ability to learn various things and in various ways. This may include verbal ability, such as ways of expressing themselves, being able to make sense of the world around them, ability to remember facts, and to take in what is being taught at school. It may also include non-verbal skills, such as being able to solve problems without the use of words (puzzles, games), the ability to observe details in their surroundings, and developmental skills such as eye–hand coordination, which is important for reading and writing.

As well as these, the EP also tries to ascertain whether the child may have any anxieties or conflicts which are hindering the ability to learn. These are often done through the use of projective tests, such as drawings and storytelling, where children can often give expression to their fears and emotional problems by using others to speak for them.

The EP also is used to assess the classroom situation and the school itself as an appropriate placement for a child. This would include determining whether they are able and willing to meet the special needs of the child, the availability of resources for children with special needs, accessibility (particularly important for physically handicapped or blind or partially sighted children), and flexibility of staff and other children. In order to make a good assessment, the EP spends time in the school, observing and speaking to the staff.

EPs are called upon to make these assessments as part of the special needs statement procedure as laid down by the Education Act (1981). Once a statement is drawn up, the school and the education authority must abide by it, and can only deviate by asking for another statement of special need to be made. Often, a child is given a statement at the beginning of formal schooling, and the EP is introduced to the family at this time. However, there are times when a child can cope with the early years at a mainstream school, with only the help the school is able to provide from its own staff, but begins to show distress or failure later. This often occurs at times of transition, for example, from infant to junior school, or from primary to secondary school, when the stresses and strains of a more demanding curriculum or a larger environment with more things to remember become too much to handle. A statement of special need can be drawn up at this time.

The statement can suggest that the child remain in mainstream, with special help within the classroom, or within the school out of the classroom. Or it may suggest that the child needs a special learning environment, such as a school for the deaf, blind, emotionally and behaviourally disturbed, physically handicapped, delicate, or learning disabled. The statement is always shown to the parents, who can make comments and disagree with the placement suggested, if they wish. They can also ask for a second opinion, if they feel the child has not been properly assessed.

The EP, as part of the job, visits mainstream and special schools on a regular basis, and schools can refer to the service when they feel a child is not coping, or when they need advice about curriculum, placement, social skills, etc. or when there are parental concerns. More formally, each statement of special need is required to be reviewed by the EP when the child is over thirteen. If there are any concerns at this time, the child may need to be reassessed.

An Educational Psychologist's training includes a good background in developmental psychology, in the emotional factors which come into play in the learning situation and in the family, in systems of education and in using consultation skills in working with schools and parents. The tools of the trade include various tests, but also observation skill, management skill and experience in education."

# CHAPTER SEVEN

# THE ADULT CHILD

## Independence

"It is ridiculous," protested Sophie, an attractive career woman in her thirties. "I run a business singlehanded, have a town flat and a country house and my mother still rings to tell me to wrap up warmly."

Whatever our parents do, the fact remains that we all remain our parents' children. Whilst adults with disabilities might have to contend with more over-protective behaviour from their parents, sometimes it is overlooked that such behaviour might not always be due to their disability. "My mother rings up to check I have got home all right," said Maureen who is wheelchair-based, "It drives me round the bend but I know she does it to my sister too and she is able-bodied and older than me."

Nevertheless, it has to be acknowledged, that whilst all children bring a mixture of worries and pleasures to their parents, the parent of a handicapped child often remains on duty as an active parent longer than most. "Jean is intelligent and reliable," said her mother. "But going out on her own she is more vulnerable. People notice she is different and they call things out."

The more severe the disability the harder it is for parents to let go of their adult handicapped children. At some levels, we have to admit that it is lucky that some parents do feel like that. Jenny is thirty-five, has no verbal speech or makaton signs and is profoundly mentally and physically handicapped. She cannot feed, toilet, dress or wash herself. She communicates bodily – clearly showing when she likes the taste of the food on her spoon but otherwise remaining immobile. Professionals are well aware that the care her mother provides is better than anything else available.

"She can't even do as much as an ordinary baby," says her sixty-five year old mother and carer. "I worry about what will happen when I am too old to manage washing her and all of that. But for now – I can do what she needs much better than anyone else." Social services have found the placement Jenny will have when her mother can no longer care. However, bright and clean as the home is and well-trained and supported as the staff are, Jenny will not be able to get anything like the close attention to her needs that her mother provides.

The situation was different for Stephanie. She was also thirty-five but only had a mild learning disability and Down's syndrome. She lived with her elderly mother who was seventy-five and physically frail and arthritic. "Mum says I can't go out in the evening because there are bad men around who would know I was different. But I know she wants to keep me in all the time because she is frightened she will have a fall."

Parents vary in how much they expect their grown-up children to be involved with them. It is quite possible that Stephanie's mother would have behaved just as possessively if Stephanie had no handicap. However, parents with grown-up children with disabilities need to plan ahead and try to provide as much independence for them as possible. Whilst there are many single adults (largely women) who have devoted their adult lives to looking after a parent (usually a mother), it is far harder for an adult with a learning disability (mental handicap) to resist this pressure.

## Grandparenthood and parenthood

Just when parents thought they had got used to their children's handicap they find friends of theirs are becoming grand-parents. This can create a sense of loss all over again which, of course, is picked up by the child, loud and clear. Sometimes, a normal sibling gets married and becomes a parent and that reduces the loss for the parent.

However, it is hard for parents to think of the deep loss their adult children are feeling, especially those with a mental handicap.

In my book "Mental Handicap and the Human Condition" (1992) I describe a profoundly handicapped young woman who was often depressed during her period. It took me a long time to realise that she was depressed because her period meant that she was not pregnant. Indeed, she had very strong feelings about not being pregnant and having to deal with the strong likelihood that she never would be and, anyway, would not be able to physically or mentally manage looking after a baby.

## Sexuality

Sexual development poses problems for parents of ordinary children. Indeed, many prefer the school to provide sex education. Unfortunately, very few schools or colleges have provided adequate sexuality and personal relationship courses for handicapped students. Indeed, all too often parents and professionals join together in wanting to forget that handicapped adolescents and adults have sexual feelings.

This joint "forgetting" extends to architects and other professionals so that privacy can become a scarce commodity in planning accommodation. In one area of London residents complained about the "inappropriate" sexual behaviour of handicapped adults at a local club. It turned out that the street and local garden square was the only place where adolescents and adults thought they might find some privacy.

Social clubs that provide escorts and cabs for those with physical disabilities often fail to allow any time between the end of the supervised activity and the club members being whisked away. For adolescents who lack the physical or economic independence to go to a cinema and sit in the back row there are few places for a private relationship to develop.

Even where families have created bedsitters within their own house or in Group Homes with private bedrooms, it can be made transparently clear that residents are not welcome to entertain guests. "Bedrooms are where you go to sleep and for when you want to be on your own. Anything else and you share the facilities we have on offer for the group," said one residential worker.

Some individuals may well end up leading or choosing to lead a celibate single life. Others may lack the emotional ability to be close to another human being. However, by denying the sexuality of adults with disabilities we damage their potential for emotional development, as when we see handicapped middle-aged women who walk about in short socks, dressed as little girls and behaving like little girls.

One of the biggest fears behind the denial of this issue is the fear of disabled adults having children. When a twelve year old is found kissing a friend no-one instantly provides detailed warnings on the dangers of pregnancy. However, it has been known for case conferences to be held as a result of two mentally handicapped adults being found kissing. There is a rush from the actual meaning of the event to fear of a terrible conclusion that may not even happen.

One young man whose mental handicap was not visually noticeable said "suppose I met a girl I liked and she liked me. Then we would go out and then she might realise I had a mental handicap and then she might stop going out with me and I would be really upset." I commented that he had not even met a girl he liked and he had already worked out what would happen. However, he was only saying in a very clear way what his parents and social worker were worrying about.

Marriages between people with handicaps have been at least as successful as with the ordinary population. Child-rearing has been at least as successful as compared with other vulnerable groups.

# CHAPTER EIGHT

# CONCLUSION

Let me return to Maureen's aims near the beginning of the book. She said she wanted to love someone, get married, have a job and a home of her own. She did.

Some people with handicaps have the ability and support to realise their aims. Others haven't. Some children with disabilities will bring pleasure and inspiration to their parents. Others will bring burdens. Most, like ordinary children, will bring a mixture of each.

Most parents manage to weather the storms of bringing up a human being without being too ground down. Where the compass isn't clear or the bad weather continues too long parents should recognise that help is needed. It may not provide dry land but it will provide support for the journey.

No family can get it right all the time. However the key to the right path is very simple. Even more than other parents you have to find out who your child is and what he or she needs. Parents vary in whether they deal with a child's talent or difficulties by taking it for granted or by strenuous action. Their own unique personalities help to determine their style of parenting. However, within the context of any particular style it is still possible to adapt to the needs of the child.

# Some final pointers.

1. A disability does not cause saintliness although we admire those rare individuals who rise above adversity.

2. A disability does not cause bad behaviour although it can deplete a child's (and family's) emotional resources making him (and them) more vulnerable.

3. A disability needs proper attention, acknowledgement and explanation.

4. Every child, whatever his or her level of disability, knows he or she is handicapped, and has feelings and fantasies about it.

5. Do not handicap yourself or your family by failing to seek support when you need it.

6. Where a child is not able to manage without the intervention of several adults, parents inherit an extended family of professionals. It is important that the team – including the parents and the child or adult – treat each other with courtesy. There can be rivalry over whose child or client someone is. Music therapy, art therapy, movement therapy, physiotherapy, remedial work, creative work, psychoanalytic psychotherapy, speech therapy, surgery, paediatrics, psychiatry, social work, volunteers are all important in allowing as much potential as possible in each unique human being to come to the fore.

# FURTHER READING

(Obtainable through Karnac Books, Finchley Rd, London NW3 tel:071 431 1075) or Nightingale Books, PO Box Shrewsbury SYI IZZ Tel: 0743 236542)

*I have Diabetes*, Althea, Dinasaur Publications

*Ben* (about mental handicap), Bodley Head Special Situation Picture Books

*Rachel* – (using a wheelchair)        "                "

*Peter gets a Hearing Aid* by Nigel Snell, Hamish Hamilton

*Ann visits the Speech Therapist*        "                "

*Claire and Emma*, by Diane Peter, A & C.Black. (Deaf girl learning to speak)

*Janet at School* by Paul White        "        (A girl with spina bifida)

*Sally can't see* by Palle Petersen        "

*My sister is different* by Betty Ren Wright.1981 Raintree (about mental handicap)

*Cromwell's Glasses* by Hally Keller, Hippo Scholastic, 1987. Visually impaired rabbit.

*Where's Spot?* by Eric Hill, National Deaf Childrens Society 1986

*Born too soon*, Office of Health Economics, 12 Whitehall, London SW1A 2DY £5


The One World Series, 1988 by Brenda Pettenuzzo, Franklin Watts, London

I have Asthma

I am blind

I have cerebral palsy

I am deaf

I have diabetes

I have Down's syndrome

I have Spina Bifida

*Give Sorrow Words. Working with a dying child*, Dorothy Judd, 1989, Free Association Books.

*Through the Night*, by Dilys Daws  1991  Free Association Books

*Mutual Respect*, ed David Brandon, 1989, Good Impressions Publishing Ltd, Hexagon House, Surbiton Hill Rd, Surbiton Surrey, KT6 4TZ (examples of how art and music therapists work)

*Mental Handicap and the Human Condition: New Approaches from the Tavistock* 1992 by Valerie Sinason, Free Association Books

*Jenny Speaks Out* by Sheila Hollins & Valerie Sinason, St Georges Hospital, Sovereign Series (Sexual abuse and mental handicap)
*Bob Tells All* by Sheila Hollins & Valerie Sinason, " (Abuse of a mentally handicapped boy)

# HELPFUL ORGANISATIONS

Afasic – The Association for all Speech Impaired Children, 347 Central Markets, London ECIA 9NH Tel: 071 236 3632 Asbah – Association for Spina Bifida and Hydrocephalus, Asbah House, 42 Park Rd, Peterborough PEI 2UQ Tel:0733 555 988

ASBAH – Association for Spina Bifida and Hydrocephalus, 22 Upper Woburn Place, London WCI

British Association for Art Therapy, 11a Richmond Rd, Brighton BN2 3RL

British Council of Organisations of Disabled People (BCODP), St Mary's Church, Greenlaw St, London SE16 5AR

British Epilepsy Association, 92 Tooley St, London SE1

British Society for Music Therapy, 69 Avondale Ave, East Barnet, Herts EN4 8NB

Cancer Relief Macmillan Fund, Anchor House, 15/19 Britten Street, London SW3 3TZ 071 351 7811

Cerebral Palsy Sport, Sycamore Sports Centre, Hungerhill Rd, St Anns, Nottingham, NG3 4NB

Community Living Team, Kings Fund Centre, 126 Albert Street, London NW1 7NF

Down's Syndrome Association, 153 Mitcham Rd, London SW17 9PG tel 081-682-4001

Fragile X Society of Great Britain, 53 Winchelsea Lane, Hastings, East Sussex, TN35 4LG

Dr Randi Hagerman, The Children's Hospital, Denver   re: Fragile   X counselling

ICSA (International Information Centre on Special Needs Education), Professor S. S. Segal, Middlesex University, Trent Park, Bramley Road, London N14 4XS. Tel: 081 362 5000

IPSEA – Independent Panel of Special Education Experts – John Wright, 12 Marsh Rd, Tillingham, Essex CM10 7SZ  0621 779 781

London Disability Arts Forum, The Diorama, Peto Place, London NW1
Telephone and Minicom: 071 935 5588

Mencap 123 Golden Lane, London ECIY ORT 071 253 9433

Muki Baum Association for the Rehabilitation of the Multi-Handicapped, 111 Anthony Rd, Downsview, Ontario, M3K 1B7 633-3971

National Association for the Dually Diagnosed: mental Illness/Mental Retardation, 110 Prince St, Kingston NY 12401

National Society for Epilepsy
Chesham Lane, Chalfont St Peter's, Gerrards Cross, Bucks. SL9 ORJ

Network for the Handicapped Princetown St London WCIR 4BB 071 831 8031

One to One, 170 Garratt's Lane London SW18 Tel: 081 877 9992
Interpersonal Relationships Project for Young People with Learning Disabilities

Parents in partnership, Portakabin by House, Blackshaw Rd, London OQT 081 767 3211

People First c/o The Kings Fund Centre, 126 Albert St, London NW1

The Parent Infant Clinic, Director: Dr Stella Acquarone, 27b Frognal, NW3 6AR Tel:071 433 3112
(This clinic was founded to understand parents and infants when they have difficulties in themselves or in the relationship with each other. This is done by individual observation of behaviour and affect attunement. In the words of Dr Acquarone, "with the birth of a handicapped baby the process of adjustment from expectation to reality is equally difficult for both parties. The baby expects food, love and understanding like any other child and the parents expect a normal happy baby. The turmoil of emotions makes the learning to know each process difficult if not impossible. The process of uncertainty before a final diagnosis is particularly eroding of the new relationship.")

PHAB (Clubs for the physically handicapped and able bodied)
Tavistock House North, Tavistock Square, London WCIH 9HX Tel: 071 388 1963

Respond. Steve Morris. Counselling for people with learning disabilities who have been sexually abused. 081 877 9992

Royal National Institute for the Blind, 224 Great Portland Street, London WIN 6AA Tel: 071 388 1266

Site at the City Lit, Stukeley Street, Drury Lane, London WC2B 5LJ 071 831 6908

Spastic Society, 12 Park Crescent, London WCI Tel: 071 636 5020

SPOD, The Association to Aid the Sexual and Personal Relationships of People with a Disability, 286 Camden Rd, London N7 OBJ

The Tavistock Clinic, 120 Belsize Lane, London NW3 5BA (There is a mental handicap workshop, autism workshop, fostering and adoption workshop and under-fives workshop)

Tourette Syndrome Association 42–40 Bell Boulevard, Bayside NY 11361 2861

Toxoplasmosis Trust, Garden Studios, 11–15 Betterton St, London WC2H 9BP

VOICE, Legal help for adults with learning disabilities who have been abused. Julie Boniface PO Box 238, Derby DE1 9JN Tel: 0332 519872

Voluntary Council for Handicapped Children, 8 Wakley St London ECIV 7QE

# UNDERSTANDING YOUR CHILD

## ORDER FORM FOR TITLES IN THIS SERIES

Send to:  Rosendale Press Ltd., Premier House
10 Greycoat Place, London SW1P 1SB

*Price per volume:* £4.75 inc. post & packing
Understanding Your Baby by Lisa Miller . . . . . copies
Understanding Your 1 Year Old by Deborah Steiner . . . . . copies
Understanding Your 2 Year Old by Susan Reid . . . . . copies
Understanding Your 3 Year Old by Judith Trowell . . . . . copies
Understanding Your 4 Year Old by Lisa Miller . . . . . copies
Understanding Your 5 Year Old by Lesley Holditch . . . . . copies

*Price per volume:* £5.65 inc. post & packing
Understanding Your 6 Year Old by Deborah Steiner . . . . . copies
Understanding Your 7 Year Old by Elsie Osborne . . . . . copies
Understanding Your 8 Year Old by Lisa Miller . . . . . copies
Understanding Your 9 Year Old by Dora Lush . . . . . copies
Understanding Your 10 Year Old by Jonathan Bradley . . . . . copies
Understanding Your 11 Year Old by Eileen Orford . . . . . copies
Understanding Your Handicapped Child by Valerie Sinason . . . . copies

Total amount enclosed: £. . . . . . . . . . .
Name . . . . . . . . . . . . . . . . . . . . . . . . . . . . . . .
Address . . . . . . . . . . . . . . . . . . . . . . . . . . . . . .
. . . . . . . . . . . . . . . . . . Post code . . . . . . . . . . . . . . . . . .